ABOVE TUCSON
THEN & NOW

By

JAMES GLINSKI

with Gene Magee's Vintage Photographs

and a Foreword by Roy P. Drachman

First Printing November 1995
Second Printing January 1996
Third Printing September 1996

© Copyright 1995 by James T. Glinski

Published by JTG Enterprise
P.O. Box 16733
Tucson, Arizona 85732-6733

Cover Design and Illustration by Corey Zimbleman

Printed by Skyline Printing
Tucson

ISBN# 0-9649387-0-7

AUTHOR'S NOTE

In the nearly six decades that span the photographs of this book, Tucson underwent an incredible transformation. An explosive growth rate set in motion a rapidly changing backdrop for its people. Quail hunting at Grant and Alvernon (Maple Ave. back then) or horseback riding near Broadway and Wilmot gave way to supermarket shopping and new car browsing. Rural resorts made way for intown shopping malls and driving golf balls replaced driving cattle in the foothills.

The area expanded so rapidly, the local joke was that city limit signs were on wheels. An example can be found in census figures: in 1950 the city of Tucson had a population of 45,454, by 1960 it boasted 212,892 residents. Sizewise, Tucson was 9.6 square miles in 1950, swelling in 10 years to 70.9. It was apparant people were attracted to Tucson's dynamic qualities. A healthy dry climate and post war economy coupled with an expanding military base and tandem industries all encouraged influx to the desert valley, as did the advent of affordable air conditioning!

For the "natives", these photographs may evoke a memory from the settings of family or personal change. For those who were not here "then", perhaps a glimpse of this era can be just as evocative, if not in interpretation, but as merely a measure of change.

J.G.
9-30-95

FOREWORD

Thanks to aerial photography and Jim Glinski's efforts to publish this book, today's Tucsonans and those who will in the future call the Old Pueblo home, can see how this great city has spread across a portion of the desert land acquired in 1853 from Mexico by the United States with the Gadsden Purchase for $10,000,000.00.

Ninety-five percent of the developed area you see in today's aerial photographs was raw desert land when I was born in Tucson in 1906. The population was no more than 15,000 when Arizona Territory became a state in 1912. At that time, most of the community was located within a mile of the present Community Center and was west of the University campus.

I remember when there was a barbed wire fence across East Sixth Street at Campbell Avenue. There was nothing east of there clear to the Rincon Mountains except perhaps a dozen scattered ranch houses.

Tucson, like nearly every other city in America, began to spread out away from the old downtown area with the growing popularity of the automobile. Nearly all families had automobiles and were free to move further away from the central city and their jobs. As Tucson began to spread across the desert, primarily to the east, shopping centers provided merchants with an opportunity to take their goods to the people, and of course all kinds of service industries followed. These were located along many of the principle thoroughfares, particularly East Speedway, East Broadway and East 22nd Street.

Tucson's growth was accelerated considerably right after World War II, particularly during the 1950's when many service men and women who had been stationed here came back to enjoy the good climate that they had an opportunity to experience while in the service.

Growth in the Catalina foothills was rather slow until the 1960's when it accelerated at a more rapid pace. For many years there were only 3 or 4 subdivisions in the Catalina foothills but in the late 1960's and through the next two decades there has been a tremendous number of new homes built in the foothill areas.

Newcomers to Tucson are seeking views of the city and views of the Catalinas. By locating in the Catalina foothills they were able to have both. That was the cause for the tremendous increase in homes on these slopes.

Growth to the northwest began to attract more home buyers because of the fact that the distances to the edge of the city to the east was so far distant from the downtown areas and from larger shopping centers. The growth in the northwestern section in the greater Tucson area has had an impact on many of the service industries in the Old Pueblo including important shopping centers.

There's no doubt that Tucson will continue to grow and I hope that it will become not just a larger city, but a better one for my grandchildren and great-grandchildren to enjoy. I'm grateful to Jim Glinski for assembling this photographic story of Tucson's growth pattern. I hope someone will continue to record the history of our town and will publish a photographic story of the Old Pueblo when one million people call it home.

Roy P. Drachman

 Downtown Tucson looking eastward with the train depot and the Carl Hayden Hospital in foreground.

 Barrio Viejo, "The Old Neighborhood", directly southwest of downtown, stands at the site of a future Tucson Convention Center.

 1946 The Miracle Mile Roadway led travelers from the north into the city center.

6

 1946   6th Avenue, looking north past the Veteran's Hospital, was the primary artery from the south.

 Congress Street, west of the Santa Cruz River, passes the city's oldest eucalyptus tree as it enters the Menlo Park area.

 1951   Saint Mary's Hospital and Round Sanatorium at the western reaches of the city.

 The University of Arizona, situated on a 40 acre plot donated by city business leaders.

The U of A football stadium surrounded by an established neighborhood.

1948 Tucson Boulevard looking north as it crosses 6th Street and a section of the Sam Hughes neighborhood.

1947 Looking east over the Barfield Sanatorium at 2110 E. Speedway, one can see the city limit is to Tucson Boulevard by the narrowing of Speedway.

c 1947 The Robert's Ranch at the northwest corner of Speedway and Swan was a rural, horseback riding stable. Notice the horsetrail along Swan.

 The view from Robert's Ranch to the southeast took in a portion of Davis Monthan Air Force Base.

1941 On Broadway, between Craycroft and Wilmot Roads, stood Brandes School, and west of it, the Wagon Wheels ranch and airstrip.

 1941 Wilmot Road looking north as it crosses Broadway. Today it is one of Tucson's busiest intersections.

1946   El Montevideo subdivision under development at the northwest quadrant of Broadway and Alvernon.

C 1950 Playing at Hi Corbett Field and Randolph Golf Course. Note: the Midway Drive-In Theatre, one of Tucson's first, in the background.

At Broadway and Country Club stands one of Tucson's premier shopping malls, The Broadway Village. The resort hotel at the right edge of photograph is the El Conquistador, site of today's El Con mall.

C 1938   Looking east of Campbell Avenue between Speedway and Elm Street is a mapped out, yet to be filled, Tucson valley.

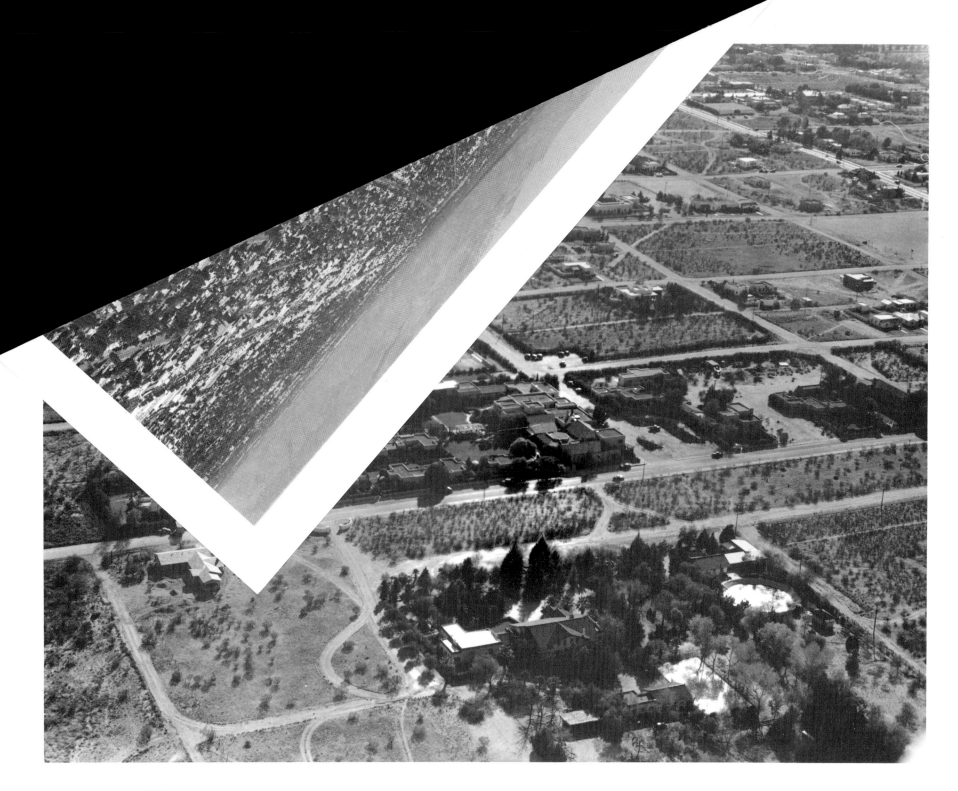

1942 Looking southwest over Potter's Place and the Arizona Inn on Elm Street, one can see the intersection of Speedway and Campbell.

1947 Grant Road intersects Campbell Avenue as a residential artery, and the Catalina Theatre stages an appearance.

1947 Looking eastward down Grant Road, a dirt Tucson Boulevard intersects in the foreground and at Country Club Road sits Catalina Junior High, today's Doolen Middle School.

1946   Fort Lowell School, on Pima Street west of Craycroft, with Tucson Medical Center in the background.

 The ruins of Fort Lowell were often a youngster's desert playground.

 Quarterhorse racing on Sabino Canyon Road at the Moltacqua Race Track and Ranch, which is The Tack Room restaurant today.

1946 The Pond's Mansion off of Speedway and Wilmot was renovated into a resort before it became a restaurant and officc complcx.

1947 At one time Soldier's Trail, off of Tanque Verde Road, was the primary access to the newly constructed highway up to Mount Lemmon.

52

Campbell Avenue going south, at the left foreground, from Blacklidge. The barren patch of desert in the southeast quadrant of Campbell and Grant was an early location for the Tucson Rodeo.

54

 1946   Gilpen's Airport at Romero and Prince Road was surrounded by a very pastoral Tucson region.

Oracle Road heading north past Reid's Desert Treasures and Citrus Groves.

1946

 A re-aligned Oracle Road at Ina, site of the new Casas Adobes shopping center.

 St. Philip's in the Hills, on the corner of River Road and Campbell Avenue.

 1941 Campbell Avenue as it winds into the foothills, looking southeast over the Rillito River.

 Hacienda del Sol resort in the saguaro studded foothills of the Catalina Mountains.

 Mission San Xavier stands at a distance from a growing Tucson.

A.E. 'GENE' MAGEE

Born in Oklahoma in 1907, Gene arrived in Tucson in 1924, and graduated from Tucson High School the following year. After earning a B.A. in Electrical Engineering from the University of Arizona in 1930, he then secured employment from Tucson Gas, Electric Light and Power Company, and later as Superintendant of Tucson Rapid Transit Company. In 1946 he co-founded Western Ways Photographic Services, where his hobby of photography advanced, and finally in 1948 started Magee Engineering, where he's been an electrical consultant to this day.

Photo by Jim Spencer

Many of the vintage photographs in this book resulted from Gene wanting aerial pictures of his engineering jobs. While he was up there in the seat of an Aeronca Chief, he'd point his World War II era K-20 camera at the Tucson valley below and capture its history as well.

THANK YOU

A very special thank you to Gene Magee for his good natured generosity of time, equipment and expertise, without which this book would simply not exist.

To Pat Corella, Rosemary Herrick and all the helpful people at the Tucson Main Public Library, for the use of negatives from their collection of Mr. Magee's photographs.

For assistance in determining dates on the vintage photos, my gratitude to Alex Jay Kimmelman, historical authority, to Laurie A. Molina at the Pima County Assessors Records, and to the good people at the Arizona Historical Society Library.

For getting me into the air for the "now" shots, my thanks to fixed wing pilot John Bransky. And for those low elevation passes gotten only in a helicopter, thanks to Fred Becker of Papillon Grand Canyon Helicopters, and Don Redman at Southwest Helicopters.

For his kindhearted acknowledgement to this project, I thank Roy P. Drachman, Tucson's longtime native son.

And to all who encouraged and supported this project, especially:

Jack Belin
Don and Denise Boulé of HRC Automotive
Mark and Shar Brumfield
Steve Byers Goldworks
Bo and Pat Collier
Clyde Hardware of Tucson
Mrs. Lew (Selma) Davis
Janet and Tom Dossin
Ted and Laura Edwards

Robert W. Finn
Sherry Fulton
Frederick William Glinski
Ted and Euayne Glinski
Grant Road Lumber
Paul Guglielmo
Larry Hayden
Andy Ingerson
In memory of Aloysius and Paula Jensen

The Kohn Partnership
Lohman's Automotive
The Magee Family
Randy Oliver
John Oper
Joe Pidgeon
Barry Rahn
Clair Read
Shirlee and Martin Reff
The Rincon Market Family

Skyline Printing
Stewart Building & Roofing Supply
Sunset Custom Homes
The Tack Room
TEPCO
Michael Thompson
Corey Zimbleman
...and to Claire, for that airplane ride.